GW00771539

Drama for Students, Volume 22

Project Editor: Anne Marie Hacht

Editorial: Sara Constantakis, Ira Mark Milne **Rights Acquisition and Management**: Lisa Kincade, Timothy Sisler **Manufacturing**: Rhonda Williams

Imaging: Lezlie Light, Mike Logusz, Kelly A. Quin **Product Design**: Pamela A. E. Galbreath

Product Manager: Meggin Condino

For more information, contact
Gale, an imprint of Cengage Learning
27500 Drake Rd.
Farmington Hills, MI 48331-3535
Or you can visit our Internet site at
http://www.gale.com

editors or publisher. Errors brought to the attention of the publisher and verified to the satisfaction of the publisher will be corrected in future editions.

ISBN 0-7876-8118-0
ISSN 1094-9232

Printed in the United States of America
10 9 8 7 6 5 4 3 2 1

Machinal

Sophie Treadwell

1928

Introduction

Machinal was first produced in 1928. It premiered on Broadway with Clark Gable cast as the lover, Dick Roe. It was a critical success and ran for 91 performances. In 1931, the drama premiered in London to some mixed reviews, mostly because of the sexual and violent nature of the play. However, *Machinal*'s greatest success came in Russia at Moscow's Kamerny Theatre, after which the play toured throughout the Russian provinces. Later, in

1954, the play was even produced for television.

The play's title means "automatic" or "mechanical" in French. Sophie Treadwell wrote the play based loosely on the murder trial of Ruth Snyder and her lover, Judd Gray, who together murdered Snyder's husband. Convicted of murdering her husband, Snyder later received the electric chair. Out of this event came the powerful, demanding drama, *Machinal*.

A woman's role during this era in history is confined and regimented to wife, mother, housekeeper, and sexual partner. Love is considered unnecessary, and thus many women are trapped in their dependant status, living a hellish life in a loveless marriage. The relationship between Helen Jones and her husband, George H. Jones, is no different. However, when a man intercedes and Helen is given a momentary glimpse of passion, her life is forever changed. She sees how society confines her, how her husband unconsciously dominates her every decision, and she feels that there is no escape. With a feeling of hopelessness, Helen commits an egregious crime, murdering her husband to free herself from the constraints of society and, ironically, to save her husband from the pain of a divorce. This heavy play is a powerful expressionistic drama about women's forced financial dependency upon men during the 1920s and their trapped existence in a male-dominated, oppressive wasteland.

Author Biography

Sophie Treadwell, an early-twentieth century expressionistic playwright, is one of the United States's most under-recognized female writers of fiction, drama and journalism. Although a productive writer, Treadwell's greatest achievement may be attributed to what she did to advance women's exposure in an oppressive, male-dominated world.

Treadwell was born on October 3, 1885 in Stockton, California. She was born to her father, Alfred Treadwell, a lawyer, city prosecutor, justice of the peace, and judge, and her mother, Nettie Treadwell. Their marriage was troubled and the two separated in the early 1890s. Although separated, Nettie never completely freed herself from her husband with a divorce. The economic and emotional impact of Nettie's inability to divorce Alfred troubled Treadwell for all her life and greatly influenced both her writing and views of marriage and society.

Regardless of Treadwell's family life, she was an excellent student and she enrolled at the University of California-Berkeley in 1902. Four years later she received her Bachelor of Letters in French.

After graduating from UC-Berkeley, Treadwell moved about teaching and trying her hand at professional theater in Los Angeles. Nothing much took hold and, in 1908, Treadwell left Los Angeles for San Francisco in order to care for her ailing mother, who was in ill health. In 1914, she was given her big break when the *San Francisco Bulletin's* editor asked her to go undercover as a homeless prostitute to see what type of charitable help was available. The result was outstanding, creating an 18-part serial which was entitled "An Outcast at the Christian Door," and inspiring the play *Sympathy*. Aside from the impact the serial had on Treadwell's writing, it also rocketed her to the fore-front of female journalists. She was sent on assignment to Europe to cover World War I, making her the first female war correspondent.

Upon her return to the United States, Treadwell began work as a journalist at the *New York Tribune*. There, Treadwell established herself nationally as a journalist with her adept and eye-opening coverage of Mexico and Mexican-American relations. One of her greatest journalistic feats was an expansive, exclusive profile of the legendary bandit, Pancho Villa. Treadwell was the only interviewer from the United States who was granted access to Villa. The two-day interview helped her complete her journalistic coup and served as the inspiration for the play *Gringo* (which appeared in 1922) and the novel *Lusita* (published in 1931).

However, there may still be one piece of non-fiction that had even a greater effect on Treadwell. In 1927, she attended the murder trial of Ruth Snyder and Judd Gray. Ruth Snyder and her lover,

Gray, plotted and killed Snyder's husband. The two were convicted and sentence to die in the electric chair. From this event sprung forth *Machinal*, Treadwell's greatest dramatic success, which was produced for the first time in 1928. Beyond the success of the play, Treadwell's characters and her sympathy for the murderess caused a stir, quietly creating a rift between conservative, disciplinarian men and a new rank of feminists.

Although her works were progressive, enlightening and revealing, Treadwell was still under the heel of a male-dominated world. Nonetheless, she persevered, pushing forward, writing countless plays, continuing with her journalism and her struggle for her place, not only amongst the ranks of women, but all humans, until her death on February 20, 1970.

Plot Summary

Episodes 1–4

The first episode takes place within the George H. Jones Company office. A young woman (later revealed to be Helen Jones) is late for work, and her coworkers chide her, telling her she may lose her job. She is a frantic woman, crushed by society. She is often late because she cannot stand the stifling crowds of the subway. This serves as a metaphor for how she feels about society in general. In the office, it becomes apparent that George H. Jones, a kind, flabby-handed, slovenly man, has asked Helen to marry him. She does not know how to answer. Helen wants nothing more than to be free of her terrible job, but the answer is a loveless marriage to an unattractive, unappealing man.

Helen returns home to discuss the proposal with her mother. At first her mother does not understand why Helen feels that she must get married. Helen even says, "All women get married, don't they?" However, as soon as Helen's mother discovers that the man is wealthy, she changes her tune, telling her daughter to marry him straightaway. Helen tries to explain that she does not love George, and her mother responds, "Love! —What does that amount to! Will it clothe you? Will it feed you? Will it pay the bills?" The two women argue, and a major theme of the play is expressed: the role of marriage and a woman's dependant status on her husband's wealth in the 1920s.

In episode three, it is clear that Helen and George have wed. They are on their honeymoon. George is not a bad person and, for the right woman, could even be an excellent husband, but he is very preoccupied with money. He does not mistreat his wife, but he also does not see her as an equal. In their hotel bedroom, George tries to seduce Helen. He is not rude or forceful, but he does express his desires, and Helen finds it impossible to resist. She has already succumbed to her role as a wife; the next logical step is to become her husband's sexual partner. Helen tearfully complies, laden with self-disgust.

At least nine months later, Helen is in a hospital having just given birth to a newborn girl. She is disgusted and depressed, feeling that the position she finds herself in (being a wife and mother) was pressed upon her by society. When the nurse asks if she wants her baby, Helen shakes her head. When George enters the room, Helen begins to gag, as if repulsed by her husband. It is only when the doctor insists that the nurse put the baby to Helen's breast that she screams, "No!" Only after everyone leaves does Helen begin to speak. In a long, rambling diatribe, Helen remembers her dog, Vixen, giving birth and how the puppies drowned in blood. Helen seems to be hoping for death and crying out that she will not submit any more.

Episodes 5–7

In a bar, two men are waiting for two women to arrive. The two men are Harry Smith and Dick Roe. Harry Smith is waiting to meet a girl from the George H. Jones Company, referred to in the play as Telephone Girl. According to Smith, Telephone Girl is bringing a friend that she plans to introduce to Dick Roe. Eventually, the two women arrive. Telephone Girl's friend is Helen Jones. Introductions are made and small talk ensues. Quickly, Telephone Girl and Harry Smith reveal that they are leaving to consummate their ongoing affair. Helen and Roe are left to talk with one another. Roe reveals that he once killed two men while traveling in Mexico. According to Roe, he was taken captive and while he was being detained, he filled a glass bottle with small stones, creating a club. At the right moment, Roe clubbed his captors to death. Roe's stories and exciting life entrap Helen.

Media Adaptations

- A television adaptation of *Machinal* was produced and aired in the United States in 1954.

In the next scene, Roe and Helen have obviously shared intimate time together. She is smitten and, for the first time in the play, talkative and excited about life. She contemplates their lives together and even sings for Roe. Eventually, she realizes that she must hurry, dress, and return to her husband. Before she leaves, she asks Roe if she can have a lily blooming in a bowl of small stones and water that sits on his windowsill. Roe agrees and Helen departs with her memento.

Back with her husband, Helen is traumatized. Both read the newspaper, and George is unchanged, rambling about sales, money, interest, and business. Helen is making comments that foreshadow suicide, murder, and divorce. However, George notices nothing. The phone rings and from the way George is talking, he is doing business and things are going well. Intermittently, as George and Helen exchange small talk, the phone rings several more times, all of the calls are related to George's business. This scene is full of heavy foreshadowing, of Helen and of George's death, drowning, suicide, and murder. George finally notices that Helen seems upset and he suggests that they take a vacation to relax.

Episodes 8–9

Episode 8 opens in a courtroom. Helen is on trial for the murder of her husband. Treadwell uses this scene to comment on the media, having one reporter obviously in favor of Helen and the other staunchly opposed. During the trial, it is revealed that Helen and George lived together for six years without a single quarrel and have had only one child, a five year-old girl. The lawyer for the prosecution asks if Helen murdered her husband, revealing that someone killed George H. Jones by smashing his head with a bottle full of small stones. Helen professes her innocence, claiming that she saw two men looming over her husband's side of the bed. The two men then smashed her husband's head and fled the room. The lawyer for the prosecution then reveals he has a signed affidavit from Richard (Dick) Roe, Helen's lover. The statement explains that Roe and Helen had intimate relations and that he had told Helen about how he killed two men with a bottle full of small stones. Before the lawyer for the prosecution can even finish reading the letter, Helen confesses to the murder. She claims that she murdered her husband because she wanted "to be free." The judge asks why she did not simply divorce her husband and, ironically, she responds, "Oh I couldn't do that!! I couldn't hurt him like that!"

In the final episode, Helen is with a priest, and she is being given her last rites. A condemned man is singing a Negro spiritual. Soon, barbers arrive to shave a portion of Helen's head in preparation for the electric chair. Helen fights them off, but the barbers prevail. In a last gasp, she screams, "Submit! Submit! Is nothing mine?" and asks the priest if she will ever find peace, if she will ever be free. Her mother arrives, and they embrace for the last time. At last, Helen is lead to the electric chair where the two reporters are awaiting her execution. In a final statement, Helen cries out her final words, "Somebody! Somebod—" but is cut short by the electric chair. In the end, Treadwell ties up her metaphor of society as a machine. Helen was caught within the machine but refused to work as part of it and, as a result, was brought to her destruction.

Characters

Adding Clerk

Adding Clerk is an unnamed male character who, in the first episode, helps emphasize and embellish the noises of the office with his audible number counting and the sound of his adding machine. Sound and noise is an important element in Treadwell's play, creating background and atmosphere.

Doctor

In episode four Helen gives birth to her firstborn. The doctor comes into the room and the nurse explains that Helen does not want her baby and appears weak because she gags when her husband enters. The doctor insists that Helen breastfeed; she refuses and asks to be left alone. The doctor is confused and perturbed by her behavior.

Filing Clerk

Filing Clerk is an unnamed, younger male character who, in the first episode, helps emphasize and embellish the noises of the office with his audible enunciation of letters as he files. Sound and noise is an important element in Treadwell's play, creating background and atmosphere.

First Reporter

In episode eight, Helen is in the courtroom on trial for the murder of her husband, George H. Jones. The First Reporter is one of the many members of the press in the crowded courtroom. As he takes notes, First Reporter reads them aloud. His comments are positive regarding Helen, her behavior, movements, character and emotions. First Reporter's comments are the polar opposite of Second Reporter's anti-Helen commentary, exemplifying the subjectivity of the media.

Helen's Mother

Helen's mother acts a guidebook for the society that Helen wishes to escape. Helen's mother constantly reminds her daughter that it is more important to get married before she is too old and that it is most important to marry a man that can provide financial stability. The old woman explains that love will never pay the bills, clothe you, or put food on the table. She tells Helen that love is not real. Life is real, things like clothes, food, a bed to sleep in, etc., and that the rest is in your head. She pressures Helen to forget about things like love, and marry George because he has money, is a decent man, and can care for both. Helen and her mother. Helen's mother is the voice that is the opposition to Helen's feelings. Helen's mother is convincing and powerful. It could be reasoned that Helen's mother's pressure is the catalyst that forces Helen into marriage, motherhood, and, eventually, murder.

George H. Jones

George H. Jones is the owner of George H. Jones Company. He employs the Adding Clerk, Filing Clerk, Stenographer, Telephone Girl and Helen Jones. He is a fat, slovenly man, but he is harmless. His hands are large and flabby; they disgust Helen. George is more dedicated to work than anything else and it shows because his business is successful. Although George's company is successful, he has never been married. He takes a special interest in Helen and decides to ask his office worker to take his hand in marriage. Reluctantly, Helen accepts, mostly because of the prodding of her mother. Helen becomes Mrs. Jones for the sake of monetary stability. She feels no love for George and, in fact, is repulsed by everything about the man. George is patient and, in a way, loving towards his new bride. He is not forceful with his sexual advances and he is eager to support both Helen and her mother. George plans to give both women a nice, comfortable life, he is willing to be faithful and compassionate, and he yearns to start a family. In many ways, George has the potential to be a good, loving husband. Soon after their marriage, Helen gives birth to their firstborn. George is excited to be a father and support his family. He is a good provider, but Helen constantly feels trapped by her husband, child, mother and life. Eventually, Helen murders George to free herself from her constraints. Ironically, she evens see murder as a better option than divorce for George because Helen does not want to *hurt* him by ending their marriage. This belief is both sad and insane. Helen believes divorce would do more damage to George than ending his life.

Helen Jones

Helen Jones is frequently referred to as "Young Woman" throughout the play. In the beginning, Helen is an employee of the George H. Jones Company. Soon she finds herself married to George and the mother of a newborn child. Helen's mother exercises a decisive amount of control over her daughter's decision-making process, pressuring her daughter to accept George's marriage proposal. Helen is a disturbed woman. She is crushed by societal norms and can find no way to escape what she sees as extremely tethering social dogmas. Helen is quiet and introspective. She seems fearful of the world, but only in that it is full of stifling pressures. She does not want to feel forced into caring for her mother; she does not want to discard the possibility of love for the reassurance of stability; she does not want to stifle sexual desire in exchange for living in a faithful, loveless marriage. Helen desires a progressive, modern feminist sense of freedom that she cannot find in her world and her life. Throughout the course of the play she succumbs to each social pressure that she is so repulsed by—marriage, financial stability, motherhood, and passionless sex—only to give herself momentary relief through an affair with Dick Roe. Their relationship is brief, but does at least give Helen a taste of a life that she felt was unattainable. Unfortunately, with Roe's departure Helen spirals into a ridiculous, dead-end choice, murdering her husband to free herself and save George from the *pain* of divorce. Of course, Helen escapes nothing and winds up in prison, on trial and eventually is executed for murdering her husband.

Judge

In episode eight, Helen is in the courtroom on trial for the murder of her husband, George H. Jones. The Judge is presiding over the courtroom and her trial.

Lawyer for the Defense

In episode eight, Helen is in the courtroom on trial for the murder of her husband, George H. Jones. The Lawyer for the Defense is defending her against the allegations.

Lawyer for the Prosecution

In episode eight, Helen is in the courtroom on trial for the murder of her husband, George H. Jones. The Lawyer for the Prosecution is prosecuting her on the charges of murder in the first degree.

Nurse

In episode four Helen gives birth to her firstborn. The nurse is in her room trying to help the new mother become accustomed to her child. Helen refuses her baby, gags when her husband enters the room, and is wholly repulsed by the world. The nurse is confused by Helen's actions and calls on the doctor for assistance.

Priest

In the final episode, moments before Helen is taken to the electric chair, Helen converses with the Priest. Mostly, she talks at the Priest as he reads her last rites. Helen divulges many of her feelings in the final episode of the play. She is extremely emotional about her forced submission into work, marriage, sex, and motherhood. The Priest is calm, collected and regimented. He gives Helen her last rites and then her head is shaved and she is led to her death in the electric chair.

Dick Roe

Dick Roe is sitting with Harry Smith in the bar during episode five. The men are waiting for Telephone Girl and Helen Jones. Telephone Girl and Smith are in the midst of an extended affair. Roe and Helen have never met, but Telephone Girl and Smith have brought the two together with the intention of a relationship beyond friendship. Helen is reluctant, as she is married and has a child, but is lifeless and dying inside because of her existence. Roe is a handsome, exciting man. He is a traveler and has adventurous stories to tell. Once, he explains to Helen, while traveling in Mexico he was kidnapped and held hostage. He had to murder his two captors and did so by slowly filling a glass bottle with tiny pebbles, creating a heavy, blunt clubbing object. Roe smashed the two men about the head, crushing their skulls and killing them both. During their affair, Helen is completely smitten with Roe and his lifestyle. After one of their trysts, Helen takes a lily in a bowl full of tiny rocks from Roe's apartment. In a strange twist, Roe's story and the bowl are the impetus to Helen's plot to murder her husband. Roe returns to Mexico and gives a written deposition that is the most damning evidence against Helen. He explains how Helen took the lily and how he told her about his daring escape from his captors. Helen's husband met a fate similar to Roe's captors and the rocks from the lily bowl were used as part of the murder weapon. Ultimately, Roe's testimony leads to Helen's murder conviction.

Second Reporter

In episode eight, Helen is in the courtroom on trial for the murder of her husband, George H. Jones. The Second Reporter is one of the many members of the press in the crowded courtroom. As he takes notes, Second Reporter reads them aloud. His comments are negative regarding Helen, her behavior, movements, character and emotions. Second Reporter's comments are the polar opposite of First Reporter's pro-Helen commentary, exemplifying the subjectivity of the media.

Harry Smith

Harry Smith is sitting with Dick Roe in the bar during episode five. Smith is planning to introduce Roe to his mistress's friend, Helen Jones. When Helen and Telephone Girl—Smith's mistress— arrive at the bar, the four individuals introduce each other and exchange bricf dialogue. Following this, Telephone Girl and Smith depart together, leaving Roe and Helen alone together.

Stenographer

Stenographer is an unnamed, faded, drying female character who, in the first episode, helps emphasize and embellish the noises of the office as she audibly recites portions of stale, business letters. Sound and noise is an important element in Treadwell's play, creating background and atmosphere.

Telephone Girl

Telephone Girl is an unnamed, cheap, amorous female character who, in the first episode, helps emphasize and embellish the noises of the office as she repeats dry, office telephone greetings. Telephone Girl reappears in episode five, where she introduces Helen Jones to Dick Roe. Helen and Telephone Girl arrive at the bar with plans to meet Roe and his friend, Harry Smith. It is clear that Telephone Girl is having an affair with Smith and, eventually, the two depart together, leaving Jones and Roe alone together in the bar. This is the catalyst for Helen and Roe's affair.

Themes

Expressionism

Expressionism is the leading theme in *Machinal*. Expressionism is a theory in art, drama, or writing that seeks to depict the subjective emotions and responses that objects and events arouse in the artist, dramatist or writer. Before exploring expressionism in *Machinal*, the term "subjective" must first be understood. To depict a subjective emotion or response, Treadwell would have to perfectly convey her personal feeling. Philosophically, it is impossible to convey a subjective emotion or response because it is inherent to each individual; it is a matter of personal taste. Hence, Treadwell cannot convey her subjective feeling to anyone because once someone else experiences her attempt to convey her emotion or response, it necessarily becomes the other person's subjective interpretation of her emotion or response. This is a difficult concept to grasp, but it is crucial to understanding expressionism.

Artistically, expressionism exists in a remarkable way. In attempts to convey their emotions, painters and dramatists did works that depicted raw and powerfully emotional states of mind. Treadwell was considered an expressionist because she abandoned the traditional structure of plays and delivered her plotlines through unique, fresh techniques. She used real events, like the Snyder-Gray murder trial and her interviews with Pancho Villa, to pour her own raw emotion into the creation of an unconventional drama. This movement is often considered decadent because it is, by its very nature, one individual's tunnel-vision interpretation of the world.

Returning to *Machinal* as the expressionistic example, Treadwell takes her subjective emotional response to the Sndyer-Gray murder trial and depicts it to the world through her play. The trial obviously stirs feelings of despair and hopelessness in Treadwell for all the women trapped in the societal norm of loveless, hellish marriages. Her emotive response to Snyder is not one of repulsion for committing a heinous act, but one of sadness for a woman left with no escape from the strangling grasp of a male-dominated society. To further accentuate her emotion, Treadwell turns away from traditionally structured theatre, constructing a nine-episode play that mimics the nine-month gestation that women must endure when they are pregnant. This is why Treadwell, and especially *Machinal*, are considered examples of American expressionistic drama.

Topics for Further Study

- Expressionism is most frequently used to describe a movement in art; however, it is also used to describe movements in drama and fiction. Examine another expressionistic work, whether it be in art or in fiction. Compare and contrast this work with Treadwell's *Machinal*. How does the use of expressionism change from one art form to another? Does the sex of the artist, author or playwright influence the use of expressionism in their work?

- Read the book *A Giacometti Portrait* by James Lord. Using what you know about expressionism, decide whether or not Giacometti is an expressionistic artist. Why or why not? Once you decide, apply your criteria to James Lord. Is Lord an expressionist? Why or why not?

- Treadwell uses the Snyder-Gray murder trial as the catalyst for her expressionistic drama. Select a moment from the past, historical or personal, and create your own short expressionistic piece. Remember, your focus should not be on realism, but on the creation of a story and landscape that best conveys your subjective emotional response to the moment.

- Beneath the shroud of expressionism, Treadwell clearly reveals her emotions about feminism and early twentieth-century male-dominated society. *Machinal* is a story about a woman trapped in a male-driven, social machine. Compare and contrast Helen's entrapment with that of Charlotte Perkins Gilman's main character in her story, "The Yellow Wallpaper." Can you think of any other works of drama or fiction where men or women are trapped, in a symbolic or realistic way, by the dictates of society?

Society as a Machine

In the play, society as a machine creates a metaphoric theme. Throughout *Machinal*, Helen struggles against society. Through Treadwell's use of sound and repeated dialogue, each phase of Helen's life is punctuated by repetition, noise, and an unseen, daunting force that pushes her along. Whether it is the opening scene in the office with the human voices creating an "office machine" or the noises of the world invading her hospital visit, Helen cannot escape society. Even though she does not want to submit, she is pushed forward, forced to carry out each of her roles in the machine—first as a secretary, then as a wife, then as a sexual partner, then as a mother—even though she hates each of her positions along the way and she continually feels pressured into submission. With this, Helen never finds a way to escape the clutches of the machine. In the end, when she tries to free herself by murdering her husband, she makes her first stand and she steps outside of her role as assigned by the machine. Almost immediately, she is devoured by society. The machine grinds her up and disposes of her once she refuses to fulfill her role. At the end of the play as Helen sits in the electric chair awaiting her death, the first reporter asks, "Suppose the machine shouldn't work!" and the second reporter responds, "It'll work!—It always works!" These statements in the final moments complete the play's metaphor. Anyone who steps outside the bounds of society will meet their end at the hands of its ever-grinding gears.

Hopelessness and Despair

Hopelessness and despair are the primary emotional themes that run through *Machinal*. Helen rarely experiences anything but these two feelings. Before George H. Jones asks her to marry him, she is trapped working in an office. When George proposes to her, she sees a relief from her horrible life in the office, only to replace it with another living hell: a loveless marriage. Succumbing to the pressures of society and her mother, Helen finds herself married, living a hopeless, desperate life. Her next role sends her spiraling into despair, as she must fulfill the prophecy of wife to become sexual partner and subsequently, mother. Given only a momentary glimmer of happiness through her affair with Dick Roe, Helen is cast down even deeper when her short-term lover leaves. Her final effort to escape her hopelessness and despair is the murder of her husband. To add insult to injury, her lover essentially convicts her with his written affidavit, leaving Helen completely hopeless and desperate. These emotions permeate all of Helen's life and serve as the driving theme that taunts her to escape her role in society.

Style

The Tragic Heroine

Although the plot of *Machinal* would seem to make Helen Jones a villain, her role is quite the contrary. She is clearly intended to be a tragic heroine. The play is written with heated anger. Helen Jones and all other women are doomed to wander the dead wasteland of a male-dominated society. Remember, this is an expressionistic play and its intent is to convey emotion and feeling, not realism. Hence, to read this play from the point of view of realism is to, of course, damn Helen to death by the electric chair and label her a villain. However, through the eyes of expressionism, Helen becomes a heroine, struggling against male oppression for all of womankind. Helen does not murder her husband because she is evil; she is left with no other choice. At the point of the murder it appears that it may be necessary for certain wives in certain circumstances to murder their husbands. With her last, failed attempt to free herself from the clutches of a male-dominated society, Helen becomes a tragic heroine.

Episodes

Structure is a crucial element in all forms of expressionism; Treadwell's *Machinal* is no different. In the play, Treadwell abandons the traditional dramatic structure of acts and scenes for nine episodes. Each episode is aptly titled to fit the setting or mood and the number is intended to reflect each month of the nine months of pregnancy.

With each passing episode, the title is the framework around which Treadwell constructs her commentary of a woman's role in a male-dominated society. In "Episode I To Business," *Machinal* opens in the office of the George H. Jones Company. The scene is bustling with office workers and a cacophony of office noises. Although it is an office, the dialogue is focused on Helen and her prospective marriage to George H. Jones. Treadwell calls the episode "To Business," but the conversation is nothing of the sort. This title is more indicative of Treadwell telling the audience what she plans to reveal than what actually happens in the episode. Through the title of her first episode and the nine-episode construction of *Machinal*, Treadwell is announcing her intention to comment on the male-dominated society of the 1920s. The episodes that follow are all aptly named—At Home, Honeymoon, Maternal, Prohibited, Intimate, Domestic, The Law, and, lastly, A Machine. The ninth and final episode not only echoes the nine months of gestation and a woman's place as a mother, it also comments on the finality of woman's place in society. The title—A Machine—directly refers to Helen's date with the electric chair.

However, Treadwell is commenting on something much deeper. With the nine episodes ending with "A Machine," Treadwell is highlighting a woman's role as nothing more than a cog in the male-dominated social machine. The play is nine episodes, just as a gestation is nine months; the ninth episode is "A Machine," just as a woman's role in society is to produce children—to be *a machine* within the male-dominated patriarchal social construct. Treadwell is surprisingly effective with her dramatic structure. *Machinal* is powerful and thought-provoking, even when viewed from afar with a unique breakdown of the general dramatic structure.

The Snyder-Gray Murder Trial

During the spring of 1927, Treadwell attended the notorious trial of Ruth Snyder and her lover, Judd Gray. Although she did not officially cover the trial as a reporter, her time spent in the courtroom served as the catalyst for *Machinal*. Snyder was a seemingly harmless housewife from Long Island, and her lover was portrayed as a dimwitted accomplice. Most notably, the trial attracted an amazing public interest and was fueled by hundreds of reporters that where assigned to cover the trial. Every day there was something new about the Snyder-Gray trial in the newspapers. The media frenzy did not cease until the defendants were finally executed by the electric chair in January, 1928. With her execution, Snyder became the first woman executed in New York State in the twentieth century.

Compare & Contrast

- **1920s:** Amelia Earhardt is the first woman to fly across the Atlantic Ocean.

  Today: Women of all ethnicities train as commercial, military, and private pilots, flying all over the world for companies, governments, and individuals.

- **1920s:** The first scheduled television broadcast airs in New York City.

  Today: Countless television programs air constantly through cable and satellite connections. Programs air in numerous languages from a vast number of networks, stretching far and wide across the entire globe.

- **1920s:** Black Friday occurs, spiraling the world into an economic crisis.

  Today: The world economy exists on a precarious balance that could easily be disrupted with war, shortages, or unemployment.

- **1920s:** Lenin, Hitler, and Mussolini all begin their rise to power in their respective countries, a precursor to World War II.

  Today: With heavy political unrest around the world, the United States is in the middle of a controversial war taking place in Iraq.

Albert Snyder, Ruth's husband, was found beaten, drugged with chloroform, and strangled in his bed on March 20, 1927. When the police arrived, Ruth was bound and gagged outside their daughter's room. She told police that a tall man grabbed her, and she had fainted. Ruth told police that she remained unconscious for at least five hours. Police were suspicious when they found Ruth's jewelry under a mattress. The house appeared to be ransacked, but it seemed strange that the thief would have left the jewelry. Secondly, when Ruth came to, she did not inquire about her husband. This also caused the police to wonder about Ruth's role in the murder and the supposed burglary. The police questioned Ruth for nearly twenty hours, and she finally confessed that she and her lover, Gray, had beaten her husband to death. Later, Ruth would change her story, stating that although she participated, Gray masterminded the entire murder.

The two were placed on trial for the murder of Albert Snyder, and the crime captured the minds of the American people. In addition to the 180 reporters assigned to the case, some 1,500 people attended the trial every day. Although Treadwell was not assigned to the cover the trial, she was a spectator as often as possible. For the first time in history, microphones and speakers were set up so everyone in the courtroom could hear the testimonies. Sadly for Ruth, her jury of peers was composed of all men, and many female reporters and thinkers of the day believed she never stood a chance. Not surprisingly, they were right. The prosecution and even Gray's defense attorney, tried to use the all-male jury to their advantage. The prosecution told the jury that Snyder killed her husband to escape an unhappy marriage, not an abusive one. With this statement, the prosecutor sealed Snyder's fate by instilling fear in each male juror, who had to begin to wonder if other wives were capable of the same crime. The jury was quick to convict and condemn Ruth Snyder to death in the electric chair.

Critical Overview

Although Treadwell was a prolific playwright and an outstanding journalist, there is still little information written about her life or plays. It is remarkable that a woman who has had successful runs of her plays on Broadway and internationally, plus had wide success as a journalist, has not received greater attention. As a journalist, Treadwell infiltrated prostitution in San Francisco, posing as a homeless prostitute to expose the lack of charitable help available to homeless women. During World War I, Treadwell was on assignment in Europe, making her one of the first female foreign war correspondents in American history. Her greatest journalistic success may have come from her two-day interview with the Mexican revolutionary bandit, Pancho Villa. Treadwell was the only American journalist granted access to Villa at his Mexican hideout.

Critically, *Machinal* was a smash success, having long runs on Broadway, in London and throughout Russia. It also catapulted Treadwell to the forefront of expressionism, making her one of the first female, American dramatists to write in the genre. Barbara L. Bywaters solidifies Treadwell's place in expressionism by comparing her to the genre's most renowned visual artist, Edvard Munch. Bywaters states her essay, "Marriage, Madness, and Murder in Sophie Treadwell's *Machinal*," in *Modern American Drama: The Female Canon*:

Combining expressionistic techniques, such as repetitive dialogue, audio effects, numerous short scenes, and the distortion of inner and outer reality, Treadwell creates, with the evocative disorientation of an Edvard Munch, the picture of an ordinary young woman driven by desperation to murder.

Although Treadwell is most often seen as an expressionist, her plays unearth prejudices and inequalities. It is fair to say that *Machinal* is a statement against a male-dominated, oppressive society; the play is trying to expose a regimented social machine that confines and defines women not by their natures, but by their husbands. However, as most critics agree, Treadwell delivers her interpretations of society through an expressionist's palate, creating suggestive, raw, emotional dramatic landscapes for her characters and plotlines.

What Do I Read Next?

- *The Yellow Wallpaper*, written by

Charlotte Perkins Gilman and first published in 1899, is a classic, haunting story about a trapped woman's mental disintegration, due largely to the oppressiveness of the society she lived in.

- *Plays* (1987), by Susan Glaspell, is a collection of plays by the early twentieth-century female playwright and winner of the Pulitzer Prize for Drama in 1931. Her plays are unique, and she is known for her refusal to create stereotypical female characters.

- *Gringo* (1922), by Sophie Treadwell, is a play that depicts and highlights the stereotypical prejudices that Mexicans and Americans have felt about each other.

- *Elmer Rice: Three Plays* (1965) is a collection from a man often held in high regard as an influential playwright. He is often noted for bringing German expressionism into American theatre.

Sources

Bywaters, Barbara L., "Marriage, Madness, and Murder in Sophie Treadwell's *Machinal*," in *Modern American Drama: The Female Canon*, edited by June Schlueter, Associated University Presses, 1990, pp. 97–110.

Dickey, Jerry, "The 'Real Lives' of Sophie Treadwell: Expressionism and the Feminist Aesthetic in *Machinal* and *For Saxophone*," in *Speaking the Other Self: American Women Writers*, edited by Jeanne Campbell Reesman, University of Georgia Press, 1997, pp. 176–84.

Tancheva, Kornelia, "Sophie Treadwell's Play *Machinal*: Strategies of Reception and Interpretation," in *Experimenters, Rebels, and Disparate Voices: The Theatre of the 1920s Celebrates American Diversity*, edited by Arthur Gewirtz and James J. Kolb, Praeger, 2003.

Treadwell, Sophie, *Machinal*, Nick Hern Books, 1993, pp. xi, 16, 17, 23, 24, 75, 79, 82, 83.

Further Reading

Dickey, Jerry, *Sophie Treadwell: A Research and Production Sourcebook*, Greenwood Press, 1997.

> This book chronicles the achievements of Sophie Treadwell, including a career and biographical overview, detailed plot summaries of her plays, criticism, and an annotated bibliography.

Jones, Jennifer, "In Defense of the Woman: Sophie Treadwell's *Machinal*," in *Modern Drama*, Vol. XXXVII, No. 3, Fall 1994.

> Jones highlights the similarities between *Machinal* and the Snyder-Gray murder trial of 1927.

Kuhns, David F., *German Expressionist Theatre: The Actor and the Stage*, Cambridge University Press, 1997.

> Kuhns traces the powerfully stylized, anti-realistic methods of symbolic acting on the German Expressionist stage from 1916 to 1921.

Styan, J. L., *Modern Drama in Theory and Practice*, Vol. 3, *Expressionism and Epic Theatre*, Cambridge University Press, 1981.

> This book traces expressionism from German through American

playwrights, including Eugene O'Neill, Thornton Wilder, and Sean O'Casey.